Creation
Everything You Need To Know.

David Gomadza

www.twofuture.world

ISBN: 9798324116194

DEDICATION

A better future.

CONTENTS

ACKNOWLEDGMENTS

Tomorrow's World Order.

EVERYTHING YOU NEED TO KNOW ABOUT CREATION

Creation
What is creation to an ordinary human being? Creation is the epitome of the world what can be Creation to you can be the end to some what is can also be that would be if we Ask the correct questions then these are the questions
What can be done
What is to be
What would be
What can be is
What would be and why
What was and why
What can be and why
What would be and when
Why and when
Why and then
Why and why not
What has been
What can be
What would be
What is to be
What can be
What could be
Now if we Ask the purpose of creation according to God here is creation
1 creation is the start of life the Genesis of everything
2 creation is creation
3 creation is why.ask

4 creation is who.why
5 creation is what but why
6 creation is what would be if
7 creation is life minus death
8 creation is death but hidden
9 creation is amen for amen means forever
10 creation is life forever without the need to ask God
11 creation is God
12 creation is life minus death plus d
13 creation is life minus ghost
14 creation is life minus heaven
15 creation is what can be but
16 creation is what would be if
17 creation is what to be but
18 what is to be is to be but
19 what can be with
20 what was to be but when
Now what has to be must be because if that is not the case then there is
no reason for living but what does this mean if we look at what can be
then we know for sure that creation is the end game in itself this is
because there is nothing without creation everything become just
because of creation those who propose other theories are doing
injustice to the power of creation if we Ask what can be this is the
answer life could be worse without hope or something to look forward
to if we Ask life what can be this is the answer life can be literary shit
this is because imagine just living for no reason?
Now that we can ask a lot of questions
1 what is to be
2 what can be
3 what is to be
4 what could be
5 what can be
6 what was
7 What can be
8 what would be
9 what has to be
10 what is
11 what can be
12 what is to be

13 what can be
14 what is to be
15 what must be
16 what is and might be
17 what would be and when
18 what has to be but when
19 what is to be but when
20 what was but how
Now what is to be must be sums up creation in that humans are created [depends from whose point of view as you will see] to die and fear death so that they live according to the creation manuals.
Creation Manual 1 God's Manual Volume 1
1 Do but ask why
2 Don't do but still ask why
3 Ask first then do but check why
4 To ask first means creation
5 To ask after means why.ask.us.when.you.created.us.ya
6 if you ask say hey how come
7 what to say means ask.why.words.ya
8 what has been said and why
9 what can be said and how
10 what can be but
11 what is to be
12 what would be
13 what is
14 what was
15 what could be
Now what if we Ask why humans were created using these questions this is the answer humans were created to obey the laws of creation designed by Yahweh if they want to go to heaven and the laws of creation by the .devil if they want to go to heaven
16 ask.why in reverse order is why.ask we must therefore ask even our self why all the time
17 to ask means godliness
18 to ask means joy
19 to joy means for
20 whom shall I send and how
21 to be near is to be near creation
22 what is to be must be according to predefined rules by .Ya

Now we must look at creation in the name of the .devil
1 creation means birth of the. Devil
2 creation means death and destruction
3 what is creation to all mankind
4 what could be creation
5 what was creation
6 what are the reasons for creation
If we look at what creation is then we can see that creation is a carefully planned and predefined activity
What could be then the answer is everything works according to a plan if it wasn't for this then creation would not work we must ask as many questions as we can and ascertain what creation is all about and these are the questions
What can be
What would be
What can be but
What would be
What could be
What might be
What if
What if but
What is to be and why
What was What can be
What could be
What would be
What has been
What might have been
What is to be
What can be
What would be
What if
When if
If then not now then when
What has been but
What can be but
What is but
What is but
What can be but
What is but

What would be but
What is but
What might be but
What is but
What would be but
What but what
What has been but
What if but
What was but
What could be but
What is but
What is but
What might be but
What is but
What can but
What could be but
What has been but
What is to be but
What buy what and then what
What would be
What could be
What was but
What is but
What what but is not
What then if not this
What would be if not this
What could be If not this
Now if we Ask again the exact questions but after what if this is the answer what if humans were not born to die but to find a way out of death then what
If makes a lot of sense only after what can we ask more to get what we want now rearrange the words in reverse brain mode [ask what could be but how]
Now what we have done is to look at every possible way and then deduce what can be deduced
What can be said about all this?
What is meant by creation did God plan to get everyone killed as an end game or creation is a way to search for some cleverness among humans?

Now let's go deeper and ask other questions and these are the questions
let's say we want to ask what can be done if we were humans and then
what that means what answer we get is not the final answer but just
half-pint meaning incomplete
Now let's Ask even more pressing questions
What can be
What would be
What is to be
What can be
What has been
What is to be
What would be
What is to be
What is but is not
What can be but is not
What is but
What but is not
What has been but is not
What would be but is not
What is not but
What could be but
What has been
What then if not now
What could be but
What has been but
What is but
What might be but
What is but
What has been but
What is to but
What has to be
What could be
What might be
What is
What is not
What might not be
What is but
What could be but is not
What is but

What could be

Now let's look at what is but is not creation is not life per se but per se life meaning indeed life without creation there is no life and if no life then there is no creation but can creation be life without life this is the answer there can never be creation without the life in it otherwise then its not creation if creation is life without life then it becomes anticipation because creation is making life what can be said about life without creation nowadays some scholars attribute life to cosmic chances in that life came about just by design not by creation they believe that God or someone did not create humans but this hypothesis did not answer clearly predefined parameters all of which ate signed with the same signature throughout .Ya I can tell you that I have discovered 978 .Ya signatures in my research about creation inside human DNA sequence here are the top 50

Iwantyoutoknow.ya

Iwantyoutoask.ya

Iwantyoutobelueve.ya

Iwantyoutoobserve.ya

Iwantyoutoaskme.ya

Iwantyoutoverifyeverything.ya

Iwantuoutoconfirm.ya

Ificanexpressmyself.ya

Whatcanbedonetohumans.ya

Ifhumansweregods.ya

Ificanbeofhelptoyou.ya

Whatif.ya

Whatcanbe.ya

Whatwoukdbe.ya

Whatwasbefore.ya

Whatcanbe.ya

Whatwouldbe.ya

Whatistobe.ya

Whatistobe.ya

Whatwastobe.ya

Whatifbut.ya

Whatwasbutwhen.ya

Whatistobebut.ya

Whatistobe.ya

Whatisya.ya

Whatwas.ya
Whatwouldbe.ya
Whatcanbebutif.ya
Whatwas.ya
Whatis.ya
Whatcanbe.ya
Whatis.ya
Whatthenwas.ya
Whatcanbe.ya
Whatistobe.ya
Whatwasthen.ya
Whatmightbe.ya
Whatisthat.ya
Whatcanbethat.ya
Whatifandhow.ya
Whatmightbe.ya
Whatcanifweare.ya
Whatis.ya
Ya.ya
[Creation manual rule 10 that says .Ya shall prevail inside all human systems so that they all know who the almighty Yahweh is and all shall confess to one another the day of the lord God that there is one mightier than the rest who resides in the clouds and as such the one who bestowed his heavenly crown on me to control and do as I shall see fit according to the creation manual 10.ya.davidgomadza.ya.ya.ya.ya.ya.ya.ya.ya.ya [X 1386976783] Signing out.Ya
Behold one on earth shall be the same as one in the skies and all shall be one until.amen.ame.amen.amen.amen.amen.amen.amen [1386976783]
If we are to ask what can be then this is what can be at one point in life one can rise to the challenge and ask all the right questions to fulfill creation so as to make one person here on earth represent .Ya for eternity having all .Ya's powers according to creation rule 10
Creation 10 as we have already dealt with it above says you shall never offer things that turn you away from the almighty instead ask.why and the heavens shall be open for you forever
Now if we are to ask what can be then this is how things can be
Yahweh can be ruthless with those who attack him

If we are to ask what we have learnt so far about creation what can this
be this is the answer creation is the best work of Yahweh meaning to
know Yahweh means to love Yahweh and to represent him on earth
Now if creation is life what then is death The opposite?
Death is discretion if that word existed but as you can see no one will
ever talk about discretion because no one will date null God's efforts
If we go back and ask what is creation then this is what we get creation
is the epitome of great works culminating in life here on earth meaning
that if in heaven then this might not be called creation
What are the rules of creation then
1 don't ask your enemy for favors that nulls your creation
2 don't ask why
3 ask when instead
4 don't vote but choose
5 don't ignore act fast
6 don't judge but take action
7 what can be but
8 don't you look down but up
9 ask when not how
10 what the fuck but how
Now what to do with creation

Ztxyztxyztttttttttttttttttt[897863862940]

Creation is the end game in itself and must be observed and respected
what can be done to have a better life
If we Ask what is then this is the truth
We can always ask Ya
We can always ask .Ya how
We can always agree with something we believe in heaven or hell its an
option but all this will determine where you go on day of death
Now let's Ask what could be what could be is that life could be the
sweetest thing ever if you know what you want if you want to go to
heaven simply follow .Ya 's rules of creation don't talk or think about
the devil but if you like to burn in hell follow the .devil,s
If we are to ask a lot of new questions then you can find out that after a
certain stage of questioning the answers remain the same heaven or hell
that means only two options either or but what need to be done to
guarantee passage to heaven If any given the fact that they are

determined by predefined apparatus
1 what to say to go to heaven answer say .Ya X 50 times per day
2 ask.why.Ya X 20 timed per day
3 ask what can be done.Ya
4 ask what was.Ya
5 ask.when.Ya
6 ask.whatcouldbe.now.start
7 ask.whatwas.ya.start
8 ask.whatifbutwhenandwhy.start
9 whatiswhatofcreation.start
10ì whathefuck.start.ya.now.start

Now if you want to go to hell this is what you must do everyday
1 you must ask the .devil

[SSoul.come.back.home.ya.davidgomadza.Ya]
Freeze in air in small crystals called Etetateteteles.start.foreverx
[1386976789]
If we are to ask what can be then this is what can be the devil can be
contacted for help
Now let's see what can be done or said if you want to go to hell
1 ask the devil for help
2 ask the devil for assistance
3 never mention acetate and questions 4 to 500 all have everything
against acetate
That means asking for acetate automatically sends you to heaven
If we are to ask a lot of questions then these are the questions
What can be done
What will be done
What has been done
What can still be done
What will be done
What can ever be done
What has been done
What is to be done
What has been done
What is to be done and when
What was and is
What can be but

What was and is
What is but why
What was and when
What might be and how
What could possible be and why
What has been done but
What is to be but how
What has been done and how what could be and why
How has things been
How could things be
But if we look at all these questions one question keeps on being answered the same no matter what what was done before that means there has never been change what was is still the same no matter what that means there is no clear cut answer or denial between heaven or hell the problem lies in frequency and extend rather that the aspect to put this in context we can tell that the brain has not evolved as much what was million years ago is still the same today the advantage being that we can easily compare things then and things now just by looking at brain scans if we are to ask the brain what could be this is the answer things could be the same but a very better life Now if we Ask what could be this is the answer A lot of things have changed and improved over the years that even if we want to try there is no way there can be another way to do things the brain over years has thought about improving things and did just that and now it has found the best there is and what is in place is the best unless if big changes occurs what can be could be as was before what is the answer this is the answer creation has remained the same people come and go and creation is still the same with same consequences and people making the same mistakes as well or some people starting to learn to cheat creation I recommend you read my other book;

33 Degrees Angle. Designing Trajectory of Death By Default.
There are other situations when the soul is trapped inside the body defeating the sole easy exit purpose of creation to avoid death at any cost and end up in heaven and not even hell hell is a failure but to who? If others choose hell when heaven is available then how can that be a failure?
1 a soul could be trapped inside the body by a simple command donotexit.start
If you start something and find out that you are stuck inside a dead

body ask .Ya for help and rescue

2 what can be said about creation must be true about heaven and hell but some souls find hell better for the fear of Yahweh who they know consume souls for eletatetetey which is something that make their bodies up

3 souls can find it hard to exit that fast as needed with the option of going to hell first and then find a way to go to heaven but with failures so far only President JFK's has managed to

4 souls can find the experience traumatizing that they rewrite the code for a much slower paced exit

What if we are to write the best code to exit the body that guaranteed a safe passage now this is the challenge that means here is a small package

1 exit safely reporting incidents and damage any issues very much prior to exit

2 ask what the hell I am stuck in here .Ya where are you

3 what can be done and how

4 what could be done

5 what has been so and why

6 what could be done and why

7 what was before and what

8 what could be and what

9 what can be and why

10 what was and why

After asking these questions what happens?

That's your destination when you die.

David is going to heaven....but David has Yahweh image meaning creation does not apply to you...live like a God ask.whatifsndwhen Nowyouareigaveyou.ya.davidgomadza.Ya.amen [136976789] [that removes human limitations]

THE FUTURE

What can be said about creation as a whole creation is a masterpiece that can never be equaled that has failed only twice in the history of mankind

1. In JFK's address of the Council of creation

2 David Gomadza's ascension but reverted as he is a representation of Yahweh on earth the proof is for all you to check ;

Ask.JFK.when.start.heavenorhell

Ask.davidgomadza.when.start.heavenorhell

Now Ask about Queen Elizabeth II

Ask.queenelizabeth2.when.start.heavenorhell

Queen Elizabeth II died and was trapped in hell under Amargeddeon II of Hell.die.forever.trapped.hugesin.forever

But pardoned by

davidgomadza.start.afterlife.elizabeth2.go.now.afterlife.davidgomadza.ya.start.ya.aproved.ya.rEaling.ya

Queen Elizabeth is alive status.afterlife.start

Now we can conclude by asking again a lot of questions critical to all this

Can people go to heaven or hell straight away regardless of actions and sins this is the answer A big no people only go to heaven If they follow .Ya or to hell if they follow .devil

Can we all go to heaven by doing good alone meaning having hell empty this is the answer If only we predefined all parameters which we did above that means we can create a stencil which everyone must use and follow to guarantee that all people can go to heaven this is possible and for the sake of future generations this is the stencil we all must use to be guaranteed of heaven

1 ask why not me .Ya
2 ask why others .Ya
3 ask what can be done .Ya
4 ask what if .Ya
5 ask what can be .Ya
6 ask why not me .Ya
7 ask what is to be .Ya
8 ask what can be done .Ya
9 ask what if .Ya
10 ask what about heaven .Ya
Now if we say this secretly in our hearts everyday and before death then heaven is guaranteed
But what about not dying at all and starting afterlife here on earth without death?
A quick davidgomadza.start.afterlife.elizabeth2.ey living organism which are part of creation to age people faster and let them die of age related diseases and these 'organism' are in every person on earth and are called or call yourselves the Permanent Makers but what if we can remove these permanent markers forever by a simple command like;
Abyss.ya.send.permanentmaker.forever.now.start.send
Now once the permanent marker has gone we can ask a simple question
Is someone like a permanent marker in here?
No answer
Now say answer as if what would be the case if we had not removed the permanent marker
I don't want I live here and trust me you still going to age and die otherwise I have no job .permanentmskerdvd.g.ended
The End

ABOUT DAVID GOMADZA

Visit www.twofuture.world